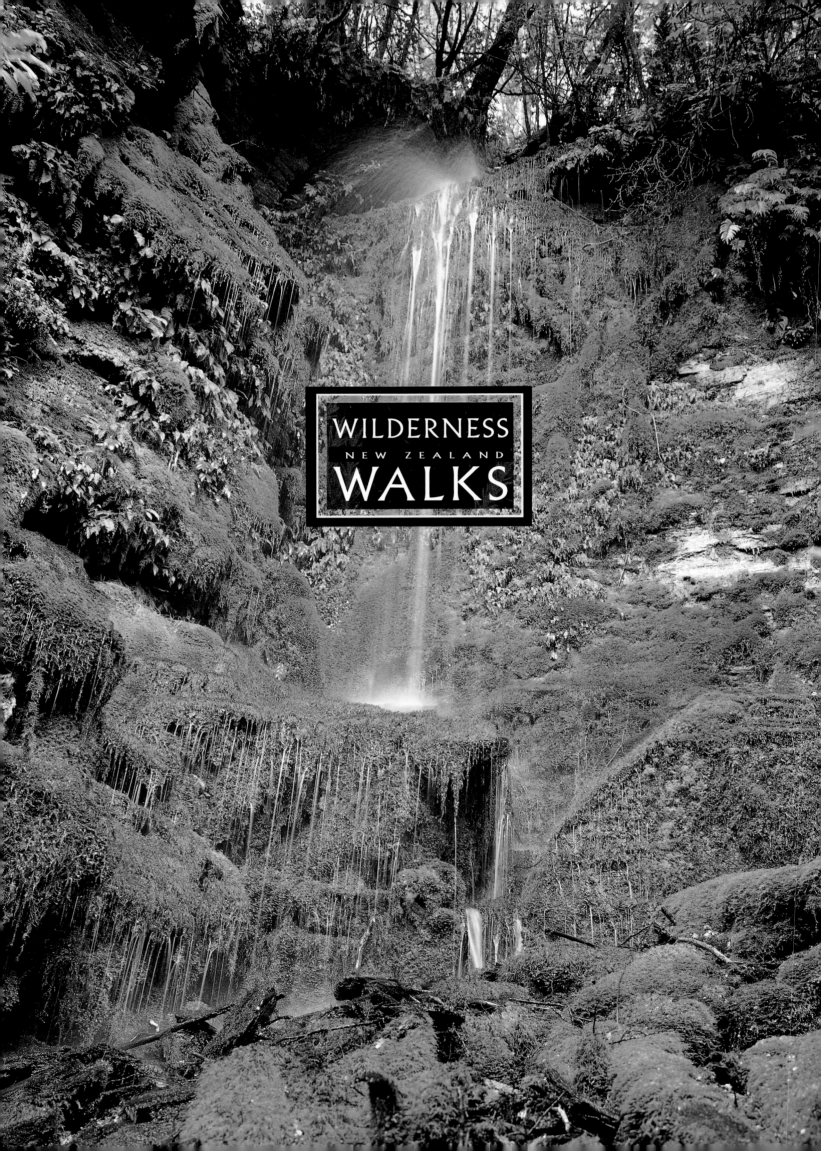

WILDERNESS
NEW ZEALAND
WALKS

WILDERNESS
NEW ZEALAND
WALKS

COLIN MOORE

Hodder Moa Beckett

CONTENTS

INTRODUCTION

The three peaks of Tongariro National Park rise above the beech and podocarp and mixed broadleaf forest of the central North Island plateau. The summits are steeped in Maori lore and are considered tapu (sacred) to Maori.

A walker in New Zealand's wilderness needs some idea of the forces which created this richly varied landscape to appreciate fully its beauty and diversity. Those who cross a steaming volcanic plateau or climb to a pass over the spine of the Southern Alps in ignorance of the country beneath their boots, or the flora and fauna around them, gain little more than a sweat. To see the surroundings as mere clumps of rock, or compostions in a viewfinder, is as unfulfilling as seeing just blocks of stone in the pyramids at Giza or in the mighty cathedrals of medieval Europe. Such magnificent structures were shaped with unbelievable energy, ingenuity and skill, and extraordinary patience.

New Zealand has its pyramids and cathedrals too. They are its mountain ranges, lakes, rivers, forests and beaches.

They too were shaped by monumental forces with infinite patience.

For millions of years New Zealand was the coastal dumping ground of Gondwanaland, a super-continent that included present-day Australia, Antarctica, South America, India and Africa. Sediment washed off the vast continent swirled and settled in the primeval sea, turning into rock under the pressure and filling trenches and basins, until finally the reclaimed land broke the surface to become part of the continent it had sprung from.

Much of New Zealand's unique flora and fauna dates from that link with Gondwanaland, but what makes the land particularly interesting is what lay beneath those sedimentary deposits, because the ocean currents dropped the Gondwanaland sediment over what would become a crack in the earth's crust.

That crack is the boundary of the Indo-Australian and Pacific tectonic plates, two of the vast plates on the earth's surface that move on the currents of its molten core like rafts of ice in a polar sea. And, just as with the ice, when they collide they buckle and deform.

Amazingly, the plate margin cuts New Zealand in half, running down a chain of fire from Samoa, through the central North Island volcanoes, and along the Southern Alps. Even more extraordinary is the manner in which the two plates meet and collide. North of Cook Strait the Pacific Plate slides under its opposing plate to create the Kermadec-Hikurangi trench in the Pacific and a line of volcanic and earthquake activity from the weakened and deformed surface.

To the south the Pacific Plate twists and overrides its

the granites on the Fiordland walks match those seen in north-west Nelson.

Gondwanaland broke up around 60 million years ago, leaving New Zealand as a raft adrift and tossed by the heaving forces beneath it. For the last 30 million years the land has had further forces acting on it: a succession of ice ages created monstrous glaciers to scour and rasp the land, continuous volcanic activity, some so cataclysmic as to be noted by Chinese and Roman historians more than 2000 years ago, and constant erosion by wind and rain.

The land has been variously submerged and uplifted, crumpled, tilted one way and moved another, its glaciers in advance or retreat. In the last three million years the central alps have risen to five times the height of Mt Cook, only to be eroded again.

Beech forest, clear streams and tumbling waterfalls, and a backdrop of lofty, snow-capped peaks —the unmistakable signature of trekking on the Great Walks of Fiordland.

neighbour along the line of the Puysegur Trench and the Alpine Fault, pushing up the land that once lay beneath the sea into the Southern Alps.

The 600km-long Alpine Fault, as straight as a ruler when viewed by satellite, is also easily recognised on the ground. Between Fox and Franz Josef Glaciers motorists drive from one tectonic plate to another around almost every bend, and the shearing force of the colliding plates is readily visible.

As well as buckling in head-on collision, the plates skew north and south. Some rock has moved as much as 450km;

All this harsh sculpture would leave a mutilated land indeed without a softening forest cover. And here is another wonder for those who venture into the New Zealand wilderness because there, on a land with the face of a geological baby, a battered raft from Gondwanaland, they will find some of the most ancient forest cathedrals on earth. The raft carried a cargo — resilient remnants of vegetation from the Gondwanaland ark survived to recolonise the modified landscape.

The bush is not just part of the New Zealand landscape, it is every New Zealander's heritage — although

Bedrock provides a sure footing in the streams of a dank rainforest.

over the years much of it has been cruelly exploited. Its ancestry is in Gondwanaland but for millions of years it evolved in isolation, in the absence of browsing animals. So the vegetation has both similarities with that found in other countries and a uniqueness derived from long isolation.

The dominant podocarp-hardwood forests of New Zealand, with their stately rimu, totara, kahikatea and kauri, are survivors of a vegetation that once spread across much of the globe. Our beeches are remarkably similar to those found in South America — and in fossils in Antarctica. Yet 84 per cent of New Zealand's plants, fish and insects are found nowhere else. Some plants, such as the giant-leaved puka, managed to survive the ice ages on northern offshore islands.

When the first Polynesian explorers arrived in New Zealand about 1200 years ago, they found a land carpeted with mostly evergreen forest. Birds were numerous but the only land mammals were two species of bat — another legacy of isolation.

The Maori's stories explaining the tumultuous creation of the land is perhaps more evocative than that of modern science. Maui, one of the quarrelsome god-children of the earth's creators, Rangi the sky father and Papa the earth mother, pulled Te Ika a Maui ("Maui's Fish" — the North Island) from the southern seas using the jaw bone of a grandparent for a hook. He fished from Te Waka a Maui ("Maui's Canoe" — the South Island).

While he rested after his mighty effort his brothers began squabbling over a share of the huge catch lying in the bottom of the canoe. They began to hack at it with their knives, and the cuts and welts they inflicted became the valleys, deep gorges and rollercoaster ranges that greet wilderness walkers today.

Whether it is the result of jealously wielded knives or the forces of volcanic fire, ice, and colliding plates on the earth's surface, the New Zealand landscape is often rugged. "Heading for the hills" tends to mean exactly that.

In the North Island wilderness walkers mostly face deeply dissected ranges, thick bush and boulder-strewn streams. In the South Island the flats of glacial valleys are usually just a pathway to high passes and steep ridges.

Of this land Samuel Butler wrote: "the land has no rest, but is continuously steep up and steep down, as if Nature had determined to try how much mountain she could place upon a given space."

And New Zealand poet Denis Glover wrote of "a country crumpled like an unmade bed".

The Greek and Roman civilisations had flourished and withered before the first humans sailed to these shores. Vast areas of Europe had already been denuded of forest and turned into pasture while New Zealand remained pristine.

Once humans arrived, however, their impact, particularly in the last two centuries, was to be unbelievably destructive. Fire, introduced animals, timber felling, and farming have all had a devastating effect.

Right: **Around every bend in the wilderness is a stream carrying water from the high country and a clear pool to tempt trekkers to bathe.**

Bottom left: **Beech — red, silver, mountain, black, and hard — is the predominant species in many walks in New Zealand forests. These magnificent specimens on the Routeburn Track are safe from sawmillers.**

Birds that had safely become flightless were suddenly at the mercy of terrestrial predators, and found their habitat diminishing. Native vegetation was often overwhelmed by introduced species, and browsed by deer, goats and possums. The fragile land, once shorn of its forests, was again riven by erosion. The legacy for future generations could have been worse but for an idea which first took root at Yellowstone in the United States in 1872, and was assisted in its growth here by the wisdom and foresight of a great Maori chief.

The creation of Tongariro as the first New Zealand National Park, its nucleus a gift by Horonuku Te Heuheu

Tukino IV in 1887, began a move to preserve and protect crucial areas of the New Zealand landscape.

It did not happen immediately; it has taken 100 years for the chain of National Parks to reach 13. But it was the introduction of the idea of preservation that was important. And the National Parks tell only part of the story.

The awakening to a need to be guardians of the land meant an awakening to the senselessness of enforced erosion, to the destruction caused by introduced species, to the foolishness of coastal reclamatiom.

The law that gives National Parks protection defines them as "areas of New Zealand that contain scenery of such distinctive quality, ecological systems, or natural features so beautiful, unique, or scientifically important that their preservation is in the national interest" which are to be preserved "in perpetuity as National Parks, for their intrinsic worth and for the benefit, use and enjoyment of the public."

National Parks have one of the most demanding conservation ethics of all protected landscapes. By law the park and everything in it must be preserved as far as possible

Along with the parks, other land was reserved or belatedly given protection so that today about one-third of New Zealand shelters under an umbrella of conservation. Most of it is administered for the present and managed for the future by the Department of Conservation.

A tiny urban reserve, containing a few forest relatives of distant ancestors, may be the simple and enduring legacy of those with the foresight to advocate setting land aside for protection. Wilderness walkers, and the trails they follow, will naturally be found, however, mostly in those vast areas inspired by Te Heuheu's gift.

in its natural state. That protection ensures wilderness walkers have the chance to see the diversity of relatively untouched landscapes, to experience peace and solitude in remote areas, to worship in the cathedrals of New Zealand and marvel at the forces that constructed them.

The range of parks is representative of the New Zealand landscape and its history. The sacred volcanoes of the Ngati Tuwharetoa in Tongariro National Park are supreme examples of the fiery force below the earth's crust that, one way or another, has had a major hand in shaping the whole country. At Tongariro this force still breaks to the surface in spectacular,

In the wilderness rivers may be as dangerous as they are visually dramatic. On the Great Walks there are bridges to carry trekkers across safely.

frightening fashion, the present overlaying the past.

The jewel of Te Urewera combines a dense forest with Glover's "crumpled bed", and the stillness and mist-cloaked valleys impart a brooding, mystical feeling. Here Te Ika a Maui is at its most mutilated — yet most magical.

To the south are the great parks where, as 17th century Dutch explorer Abel Tasman noted, the land has been "uplifted high". It would be too much to expect him to appreciate that the land had also been sheared south to north, that in the Abel Tasman and Kahurangi National Parks would be rock once adjacent to that in the far south of Fiordland.

In Abel Tasman the corrosive force of water leaves behind lagoons framed by golden sands that were once part of the granite and marble landscape.

plates. The pile soars into snowbound heights; for every centimetre it rises, the forces of ice and water will scour it down. Ice has done almost as much as the earth's fractious crust to shape these areas. Great glaciers formed during the ice ages rasped away at the rock as they slowly flowed off the mountains. When the earth warmed and the glaciers retreated they left deep valleys to show their passing, some hanging high in the mountains, others filled with water to become lakes and fiords.

In these parks are the pages of a geological textbook, open for all to see. The sediment squashed into rock, then tipped or folded, are the slopes that walkers may climb. Easily visible too is the formidable artillery of erosion. There are piles of rubble left by bulldozing glaciers, scree slopes left by freeze and thaw, wind and rain, and avalanche. Rivers

Shelters on the high passes provide a place to rest, get warm, and sometimes, take shelter from unfriendly alpine weather.

At Kahurangi the water works its way through limestone karst plateaus and mountains to fashion an underground plumbing system that dramaticallly demonstrates the infinite patience of New Zealand's pyramid builders. In these caverns are preserved fossil imprints of Gondwanaland, examples of the earliest species to make a home on the compacted sediment. Preserved in these caves too are the remains of moa, giant flightless birds that evolved in the security of an island and were easy prey to the first human hunters.

In the Mt Aspiring and Fiordland National Parks is the imposing mountains of rubble left by crashing tectonic

plough the land, carrying great masses of it with them when they are violently in flood.

Stewart Island, the anchor stone for Maui's canoe, is not a national park, but much of it is preserved because it is part of the same textbook.

Humans have travelled through these lands for more than a thousand years. Maori settlers explored their new country and found the best routes through it. They used rivers and streams as pathways into some of the more rugged areas, and discovered the lowest, and therefore safest, passes across the mountains. When the first Europeans arrived they were to use many of the trading routes that the Maori had established.

In Europe it was the British who pioneered the notion of wilderness walking. They took climbing for pleasure to the alps of Europe and introduced the idea to people who had previously climbed mountains only because they grazed stock on them or had to cross them in their travels from one place to another.

When British settlers arrived in New Zealand they brought the pastime of wilderness walking with them. Within a few years clubs were formed to encourage the activity, and organisations sprung up to lobby governments to conserve the wilderness they wanted to explore. Without their efforts much of the wilderness enjoyed today would not have been preserved.

On raft New Zealand the walkers were modified by the landscape too. They became trampers. They learned to carry loads on their backs so they could be self-sufficient in an unpopulated land. They learned bushcraft so they could survive in a country where navigation was fraught with uncertainty. And they learned how to be safe in a land subject to notoriously changeable weather, where the two greatest dangers for walkers are exposure and drowning in flooded rivers.

The trampers did something else too; they established and popularised some major trails. These were tracks that traversed the most interesting, if not challenging, terrain in the wilderness.

Every protected area of this hugely diverse country was to become crossed by a tramping track, and a tramping culture for walking them evolved. Huts were built along the way. And today thousands of people walk them, many from overseas.

In 1992 the Department of Conservation classified

eight of the tracks as Great Walks and upgraded the standard of the tracks and their huts. The walks are not necessarily the best of what New Zealand tramping has to offer; they were designated as Great Walks because they were the most used, particularly by overseas visitors, and because they undoubtedly crossed the most spectacular and most representative landscapes in New Zealand.

Other tracks may be more demanding, more secluded, and less accessible, but none has greater or more inspiring scenery, or more significant and fascinating history than the eight Great Walks.

"Walks" is something of a misnomer because these are tracks in the New Zealand wilderness. Many are alpine routes where the weather strikes with a fatal ferocity to take the lives of the unprepared. Yet none of the Great Walks is beyond the ability of ordinary, healthy people of average fitness who take care to follow New Zealand tramping advice, especially on clothing and equipment.

New Zealand Wilderness Walks is intended to inspire people to make one, or all, of these Great Walks; to see and touch the pyramids and cathedrals of New Zealand; to feel the great forces of nature at work.

A companion volume, *New Zealand's Great Walks* by Pearl Hewson, serves as a valuable field guide, with hut-to-hut descriptions of all the walks, for those who are inspired.

This book is also intended as a lasting record of these great New Zealand tracks, a momento, as well as an insight into the creation of this land and the people who have settled it and preserved some of its wilderness — and its Great Walks. Happy tramping.

COLIN MOORE

The muted colours and tranquillity of a wilderness sunset bring another day to a close on a New Zealand Great Walk.

TONGARIRO

Fire and ice have shaped the landscape of the Tongariro Northern Circuit — and still do. Walkers climb warily past the still active Red Crater and its unusual vertical dyke formed when a lava flow drained back into it. Steam and gases from the crater condense into the cold waters of the Emerald Lakes to create their milky appearance.

Horonuku Te Heuheu Tukino IV, paramount chief of Ngati Tuwharetoa, strode to the window of the courtroom and looked across the waters of Lake Taupo to his sacred mountains. The chief carried the mantle of the ancient proverb "Tongariro the mountain; Taupo the sea; Ngati Tuwharetoa the tribe; Te Heuheu the man." His father had refused to sign the Treaty of Waitangi and cede sovereignty to the British Crown. And now his kai tiaki (guardianship) of the land was under challenge by another chief attempting to exploit the arrival of the Pakeha's "land courts".

The rival chief claimed raupatu (conquest) rights and said he had kindled his ahi ka (fires of occupation) on the territory.

"Look yonder," thundered Te Heuheu, pointing across the lake to where a coil of vapour rose from a distant summit. "Behold my ahi ka, my mountain Tongariro. There burns my fire kindled by my ancestor Ngatoro-i-rangi. It was he who lit that fire and it has burned there ever since. That is my fire of occupation. Now show me yours." Those compelling words — "Behold my fire!" — are inseparable from the Tongariro National Park and the Great Walk that winds its way between the three commanding volcanic peaks of the central North Island.

It is fortunate that Ngati Tuwharetoa held these mountains sacred because, when they appeared threatened by land-hungry European immigrants, Te Heuheu Tukino secured the mana of his tribe and his ancestors for all time by gifting the peaks as the nucleus of the world's fourth National Park.

The initial gift of 2600ha has been steadily added to, and now totals 76,0000ha. The park is recognised by UNESCO as a World Heritage site and one of only 17 in the world to receive that status for both its environmental and cultural significance.

The peaks, all relatively young in geological terms, are no ordinary volcanoes. In Maori mythology they are the first offspring of Papa, the earth mother, and Rangi the sky father.

Once warrior gods stood here and fought over the love of beautifully rounded Mt Pihanga. Tongariro won her in fierce combat and sent his rival Mt Taranaki fleeing to the west and Tauhara and Putauki to the north.

Centuries later came the Arawa canoe and its navigator and high priest Ngatoro-i-rangi, ancestor of the Ngati Tuwharetoa, who climbed Ngauruhoe to spy out the new land. At the summit he was enveloped in a sudden, and unfamiliar, snowstorm. Frightened and frozen he cried out to his priestess sisters in Hawaiiki for help: "Ka riro au i te tonga. Haria mai he ahi moku." (I am borne away by the cold south wind! Send fire to warm me.)

In response a volcanic fire came by way of smoking White Island, Rotorua and Taupo, before bursting forth on Ngauruhoe to warm Ngatoro.

Modern science has a no less dramatic explanation for Te Heuheu's ahi ka. Fire runs down the length of the perforation in the earth's surface caused by the clashing of the Indian-Australian and Pacific Plates, all the way from Samoa. At Tongariro the weakness caused by the colliding plates allows the molten core to spew out of the earth. What gives the Tongariro volcanic complex its special status is that the activity is relatively recent. It is also ongoing. Walkers on the Tongariro Great Walk may observe the past, present and future. They are part of a world that is literally in the making.

They will traverse lava flow valleys too young to be colonised by anything but the most basic of plant life, pass old explosion craters and those still steaming and smoking, and tread rock and ash that have been ejected from the bowels of the earth.

Despite its common volcanic origin the terrain covered by the Tongariro Northern Circuit is extraordinarily diverse. Even the mountains are quite different in character. Ruapehu is a massif with several peaks, a crater 1.5km in diameter, a hot crater lake, ice cliffs, mud and lava flows decorating its flanks, and many glacially carved gullies.

Ngauruhoe is a classic andesite cone, its steep sides constructed by intermittent eruptions from a central vent. And Tongariro is a multiple volcano composed of a number of vents, some quite recent and some from its earliest beginnings.

The track around the complex is not a true circuit in that to complete it requires retracing some steps. It basically encircles Mt Ngauruhoe with an entry or exit either over Mt Tongariro or over the tussock grasslands to the east of Mt Ruapehu.

The three mountains of the central North Island, dressed in mid-winter snow, draw skiers and ski-tourists to the wilderness tracks.

Most walkers, however, join the circuit at the beginning of the Mangatepopo Valley and the start of the Tongariro Crossing, an eight-hour walk across the mountain that is considered to be one of the best one-day walks in New Zealand.

An ice-age glacier once filled the valley and the moraines it left are clearly visible. More recently lava has flowed down the valley, particularly towards its head, where it rises into a steep saddle that connects Mt Ngauruhoe and Mt Tongariro.

This is a rocky, gut-busting section of the trail but the reward at the top of the Mangatepopo Saddle is a stunning view back down the valley, perhaps all the way to Mt Taranaki in the west.

From here there is a poled route to the 2291m summit of Ngauruhoe. The volcano in its present striking form is only about 2500 years old. A massive eruption in 1954 sent an estimated eight million cubic metres of lava flowing towards the Mangatepopo Valley. Some of the flows were more than 18m thick and still warm a year later.

Wisps of smoke and steam still rise from the Ngauruhoe crater. The climb to the crater rim over loose volcanic debris can be a frustrating exercise of one step back

A short track from here leads to the summit of Tongariro. Below are the Emerald Lakes, the wide expanse of Central Crater, and the route around the eastern flanks of Tongariro to the Ketetahi Hut and Ketetahi Hot Springs.

The path of lava flows from the Te Maari craters is clearly evident through the Okahukura Bush. The track, however, follows a more northerly, tussock-clad ridge until it reaches the bushline and a well-formed path to the Ketetahi Track road-end. Alternatively, the Northern Circuit heads east from Emerald Lakes, descending into the Oturere Valley, a spectacular moonscape first carved by a glacier and then sculpted by lava flows, up to 30m thick and 400m wide, from Red Crater. The lava here has cooled to form an endless variety of weird-shaped lumps.

Fireballs explode into the sky during the 1996 eruption of a restless Mt Ruapehu, which added yet another layer of ash to the volcanic wilderness.

Between the Oturere Hut and the Waihohonu Hut are loose gravel fields that plant life struggles to recolonise. It is definitely desert-like; the cause is not so much lack of water as frequent strong, dry winds.

A healthy beech forest has successfully colonised the broad Waihohonu Valley and the Waihohonu Hut sits among the trees. Across the stream is the original Waihohonu Hut, built by the government in 1901. The hut, preserved as an historic building, was the first centre of tourist activity at the mountains and carved into its beams are the names and initials of generations of trampers.

for every two forward.

The large basin that separates Tongariro from Ngauruhoe is called South Crater, although it has more likely been formed by glacial erosion. It does contain at least one explosion pit that in early summer becomes a pool of water from melted ice and later dries into a cracked mud mosaic.

A steep lava wall at the head of the basin leads up to the still active Red Crater and perhaps the most inspiring feature of the Northern Circuit. To look down into this many-hued vent is to peer into volcanic creation.

From the old hut the Waihohonu Track follows the stream through mountain beech forest and then alpine tussock onto the Tama Saddle. Like the Tongariro Crossing, this is exposed and windy in bad weather and should not be attempted without suitable clothing.

Tama Lakes, two 10,000-year-old explosion craters, the largest in the park, lie in the high saddle between Ruapehu and Ngauruhoe. In Ngati Tuwharetoa mythology the craters were left when Mt Taranaki was banished to the west.

Whakapapa Village is a couple of hours' walking further on. The full Northern Circuit — and circumnavigation of Ngauruhoe — is completed by turning north at Taranaki Falls on the Wairere Stream and following the western foothills of Mt Ngauruhoe to the Mangatepopo road-end.

Below: **E**ven volcanic rubble is rarely desolate as mosses and lichens softly clothe the rocks, and plants like the mountain daisy adapt to colonise the previously harsh landscape.

Left: **M**t Ruapehu belches smoke and steam into the sky above the Wairere Stream which carries meltwater off the mountain's northern slopes down the Wairere Valley. Walkers on the Northern Circuit cross the stream soon after leaving Whakapapa village.

TONGARIRO

Overleaf: **T**ama Lakes lie in 10,000-year-old explosion craters on the high saddle between Mt Ngauruhoe and Mt Ruapehu that is crossed by the Waihohonu Track. The upper and lower lakes are known as Nga Puna a Tama or the springs of Tama. The lakes were named after Tamatea, the high chief of the Takitimu Canoe, who explored the area 600 years ago. The lakes are also home to a seagull colony, many kilometres from the ocean.

From Ketetahi it is possible on a clear day to imagine, if not see, beyond Lake Rotoaira and its small lava island of Motuopuhi, past Mt Pihanga and Lake Taupo, the pulsating heart of Maui's fish, to Putauaki (Mt Edgecumbe), smoking White Island, Raoul Island and the volcanic islands of Tonga and into the Pacific Ocean for 2500km along the colliding plates of the earth's crust, known as the Pacific Ring of Fire.

Below: **K**etetahi Hot Springs on the northern slopes of Mt Tongariro lie in small enclave within Tongariro National Park that has been retained in Ngati Tuwharetoa ownership because of its cultural importance to the tribe. There are more than 40 fumaroles among the boiling springs and mud pools with the largest discharging steam heated to about 138°C. The Tongariro Crossing passes through the springs area with the permission of its Maori owners.

TONGARIRO

Overleaf: **T**rampers wind their way across the floor of desolate Central Crater between Red Crater and the saddle, to Ketetahi and the northern slopes of Tongariro. The 1km-wide basin has no recognisable vent and despite its shape and name is not likely to be a crater at all. Mt Ngauruhoe, and in the distance Mt Ruapehu, form a line to the south.

Left: **T**rampers pause near the summit of Red Crater to look beyond Central Crater to Blue Lake Crater where cold, blue-tinted water fills an inactive vent. The lake was originally called Te wai-whakaata-o-Te Rangihiroa (Rangihiroa's Mirror) in honour of one of the ancestors of the Te Heu Heu family. Overlooking the lake is the hill Rotopaunga and, in the far distance, Mt Pihanga.

TONGARIRO

Bottom left: **M**inerals leaching out of Red Crater, particularly sulphur and ammonium chloride, give the Emerald Lakes their distinctive hue. The lakes are cold despite nearby steam vents. Across the saddle in the distance lies the Oturere Valley and the route to Waihohonu.

Overleaf: **A** winter mantle covers Mt Tongariro, with North Crater in the foreground, Mt Ngauruhoe, and the Ruapehu massif in the distance. When the snow is thick it is possible to make the Tongariro Crossing between Ngauruhoe and Tongariro on touring skis and to climb and ski the challenging slopes of Ngauruhoe.

Right: **W**inter sculpts its signature on the margins of the Mangatepopo Stream, which is carried in meltwater channels off the southern slopes of Tongariro. The Mangatepopo Track across Mt Tongariro follows the stream to near its source at Soda Springs.

TONGARIRO

Above: **D**oing the dishes at Oturere Hut, one of four huts maintained by the Department of Conservation on the Tongariro Northern Circuit. The huts are equipped with bunks and mattresses, gas cookers, gas heating, a water supply and toilet facilities. Passes for the huts must be purchased in advance. Oturere, sited near the bottom of the bleak Oturere Valley, is one of the least used, but with an impressive Mt Ngauruhoe backdrop is one of the more interesting hut locations.

Overleaf: **S**torm clouds roll in to veil the summits of Mt Tongariro and Mt Ngauruhoe and touch the low cone of Pukekaikiore as a party of trampers retreat from the Mangatepopo Valley across the tussock and heather of the central plateau. In flower the heather turns these grasslands a delicate mauve, but it is an introduced pest that, if left unchecked, will suffocate the native grasses.

WAIKAREMOANA

Mystical Waikaremoana, the "sea of rippling waters" high in the Urewera Ranges, is fed by many bush streams that must tumble over a tortured landscape. Aniwaniwa Falls is near the Urewera National Park Headquarters, first point of call for walkers on the Lake Waikaremoana Track.

There is something mystical about Lake Waikaremoana, nestling high in the Urewera Ranges on the eastern bulge of the North Island.It is felt even before travellers first glimpse the "sea of rippling waters" through the trees on the edge of State Highway 38 to Wairoa. The feeling begins at Te Whaiti at the entrance to the riven ranges of the 212,000ha Te Urewera National Park and its dense bush.

As light and a gentle breeze play on the bush beside the mainly unsealed and perversely winding road across the Huiarau Range, there is a sensation of not being alone. This is the Urewera, ancestral home of the Tuhoe, the Children of the Mist, and in the deep bush there is an ethereal but unmistakable presence.

This is the land that gave succour to warriors and prophets like Te Kooti Arikirangi Te Turuki and Rua Kenana, who fought the government of the day.

Seen through the roadside trees, on the southern shore of the lake, is the brooding bulk of Panekiri Bluff, a huge uplifted block of sedimentary rock that brings the Panekiri Range to an abrupt end 610m above the lake waters.

The Lake Waikaremoana Track, the second of New Zealand's Great Walks in the North Island, nears its end in the goblin forests on the heights of Panekiri Bluff. And up there too the celestial Mist Maiden, Hine-pokohu-rangi, mother of the Tuhoe, swirls around the moss-sheathed boughs of twisted beech trees and often hides the lake beneath her shimmering robes.

An ancient river once flowed at the foot of the bluff until a thrashing taniwha, or water monster, Haumapuhuia, tore at the earth in a desperate bid to reach the sea, carving out great channels and hollows where water flowed to form the second largest lake in the North Island. Or, if you prefer, it was the work of an earthquake and a huge landslide about 2200 years ago that dammed the Waikaretaheke River and drowned an ancient forest in the valley system behind it.

But the mist-wreathed hills and valleys of Te Urewera National Park that surround the lake are steeped in Maori lore and legend, home to the Patu-paiarehe, the fair-skinned fairy people, or forest elves. Sometimes when the Mist Maiden comes up to embrace her lover, Maungapohatu, the sacred mountain, travellers can hear the Patu-paiarehe singing and calling to them in the goblin forests of Tane.

There are likely to be other voices in these mystical forests. Some 10,000 people, including overseas visitors, come each year to walk the 46km track carved around the lake's southern and western shores in the mid-1960s by volunteers, many from North Island secondary schools.

The highway from Rotorua to Wairoa runs virtually north to south down the lake's eastern shore and the lake track runs from the most northern and southern points of the foreshore road — it can be walked in either direction — to complete an encirclement of Waikaremoana.

Once the lake track became so popular that it was in danger of being loved to destruction. Scrub and sizeable trees were cut indiscriminately for firewood and to clear campsites, poor toilet hygiene fouled the lake shore, and in many places the track was turned into a bog.

Mud is almost inevitable on any track in the Ureweras. Since its designation as one of the country's Great Walks, however, the Lake Waikaremoana Track has been granted a $1 million, eight-year upgrading programme.

The track is served by five huts, four on the lake shore and a new 36-bunk hut at Puketapu, at 1180m the highest point on the Panekiri Range. The site must rank as one of the best in the Great Walks' network: from the hut's expansive decks there is a spectacular view of the deeply

indented lake and the forested ranges beyond. The hills have been shaped by a process of continuous erosion — this is an area of high rainfall — to form countless ridges and valleys.

Birdlife is abundant in the mainly podocarp mixed broadleaf forest around the lake. On the heights of Panekiri there is montane beech forest and the unmistakable flora of alpine regions.

In the winter snowfalls are not uncommon and the gas heaters installed in the huts are there as much for safety as comfort. The huts have a water supply, toilet facilities and heaters, but no cooking facilities; walkers must bring their own portable cookers.

Early morning tranquillity on Waikaremoana.

The track upgrading has included the creation of designated campsites, with water supplies and toilets, and handsome shelters in the design of a Maori whare, where campers can unpack out of the weather and set up portable stoves for cooking.

Carved into the lintel of the shelters and on signs and information boards elsewhere is the Lake Waikaremoana Track motif, a stylized interpretation of Hine-pukohu-rangi. It is appropriate to remind walkers that the Mist Maiden, mother of the Tuhoe, is never far away because the Tuhoe left

Korokoro Falls are just a short walk from the Lake Waikaremoana track.

no corner of their remote forest unexplored. Many of their spiritual and cultural traditions remain closely linked with the Urewera forests which, isolated from the sea and fertile food-crop land, they depended on for food and clothing.

Nowhere is tradition more evident than around the Lake Waikaremoana Track. It loosely follows a route used by the Maori for many centuries and in many places crosses tiny enclaves of private land. The lake area was the scene of many bloody and gruesome battles between Tuhoe and Ngati Ruapani; many of the private areas were places of grisly slaughter or are burial grounds. These places are regarded by Tuhoe as extremely sacred and so were withheld from the park. Walkers are requested to stay on the track when near them.

Apart from the slog up Panekiri Bluff — a grind worth every single step — the Lake Waikaremoana Track is on easy ground, making it one Great Walk where age or tramping experience can never be considered an impediment.

Sometimes the families of three generations tackle the track and make use of a special feature of the Waikaremoana walk. It is possible to use a dinghy as a supply boat, or relief transport, and to meet the walkers at one of four huts along the way. Some of the most lavish meals in the New Zealand backcountry, perhaps served with a selection of fine wines, are prepared in the huts of the Lake Waikaremoana Track — the food all ferried by boat.

There is a downside to such indulgence, however. The lake is subject to some of the fiercest and most sudden storms imaginable. As the wind accelerates off the steep ranges and funnels down the lake inlets it turns the water into a maelstrom to rival anything an angry taniwha could produce.

The Maori who used the lake extensively as a transport route had a considerable fleet at Waikaremoana and the lake storms took their toll on open canoes. European boats are just as vulnerable to the sudden gales. Anyone ferrying supplies for walkers must be prepared to sit tight when the wind starts to blow through two potentially lethal traps, the entrance to the Whanganui inlet and Te Kauanga O Manaia (the Narrows), the treacherously narrow entrance to Wairaumoana (the Wairau Arm).

The lake shore route of this Great Walk has another bonus — trout. At certain times, particularly November, trout feed in the shallows where weedbeds separate the shore from deeper water. The fish are often visible or it can be seen where they are feeding, and an accomplished flyfisher can add fresh trout to their hut menu. There are both rainbow and brown trout in Lake Waikaremoana but the lake is known particularly as a quality brown trout fishery.

Kayakers and hunters also use the huts on the lake track; it is not unknown for a foreign tramper (if anyone back home would believe such a tale) to be treated to trout, wild pork and wine by others using the huts.

A Tuhoe saying advises people to go to the mountains to be cleansed by the winds of Tawhirimatea, god of storms. There may be no better way for a spiritual reassessment and personal reawakening than to spend five days around the shores of Lake Waikaremoana, in the primeval forests of the Ureweras, and in the bosom of the Mist Maiden on Panekiri Bluff.

Previous page: Thick bush, distant ranges and a rippling lakeshore — the ever present companions on the 46km Lake Waikaremoana Track. One of several inlets along the trail.

WAIKAREMOANA

Below: The 18-bunk Marauiti Hut nestles on the edge of the bush in Marauiti Bay. The swampy flats in the bay attract many native birds to gorge on the prolific insect life or the nectar-rich flax flowers.

Above: Trampers pause to admire a tranquil lake and their route that lies ahead around the shore. Wind accelerating off the ranges and down the lake arms can quickly turn these quiet waters into a dangerous cauldron.

Below: In places the trail onto the heights of Panekiri bluffs needs the help and safety of a wooden stairway or a knotted rope to ease the climb.

Overleaf: The Panekiri Bluff, a huge uplifted block of sedimentary rock that brings the Panekiri Range to an abrupt end at Lake Waikaremoana. The bluff, 1177m above sea level at Pukenui, its highest point, rivals the lake as the dominant feature of the Great Walk around Lake Waikaremoana.

Left: **T**here are few more commanding views in the North Island bush than that from Panekiri Bluff. From its highest point the indented Lake Waikaremoana is 600m below.

Above: **D**awn at Maraunui Bay has a special magic as the Urewera mist hangs on the ranges and a lone fisherman casts for a trophy brown trout in the still water.

ABEL TASMAN

Sand, sea and a lushly forested foreshore on the Awaroa inlet; the unmistakeable elements of Abel Tasman National Park and a Great Walk that can be a great paddle for bare feet and kayak too.

Tucked into the north-west tip of the South Island is a New Zealand icon. The 22,139ha Abel Tasman National Park, the smallest in the country, was likely never thought of as such when it was opened in 1942, 300 years after the visit of the Dutch navigator who gave New Zealand its modern name.

The coastal park's conservation values are not in question; those have been recognised as special since Nelson conservationist Perrine Moncrieff first began campaigning against logging the coastal forests in 1941.

But it has taken the more recent arrival of thousands of backpackers, and the designation of a path along the park's coastline as one of New Zealand's Great Walks, to forge an image of the Abel Tasman park that is like no other in the country. Other walks boast pristine New Zealand bush, clear streams, and fresh lakes. Some touch the coastline too. But the honey-coloured sand beaches of Abel Tasman, and brilliant aquamarine and turquoise seas, together with a backdrop of lush green bush, are unique.

There is a hint of the tropics and coral atolls — except that in places seals laze on the rocky foreshore. The land behind the sands is confusing too. It is mostly granite and the landscape can be bizarre, inviting in one place and aloofly resistant in others.

The Abel Tasman Coastal Track follows 38km of easy-graded walking from Marahau to Totaranui, with a further 13km to Wainui Inlet, and encapsulates most of the natural values of the park.

This is a track that can be safely walked — in either direction — in running shoes, where there are quiet, safe-swimming coves to linger at, perhaps for a day or two. It is possible to enter or exit by boat at several points, or paddle a kayak one way and return on foot the other.

Given its convenience, beauty, and many options — and the amiable weather of the Nelson region — it is hardly surprising that the track is one of the most commercially prized of the Great Walks. Yet that does not detract from the walk; it just opens up further opportunities to enjoy its features. Aqua taxis for hikers, daily coach services to and from the track road-ends, seal and dolphin watch tours, and sea kayak hire all increase the possibilities to experience an icon.

At times it can almost get suburban, with videocamera-packing daytrippers hopping off the morning ferry to walk to the next bay before being picked up. But this is a place that is a pleasure to share.

It wasn't always so. When Abel Tasman anchored off these shores on 18 December 1642, having survived a West Coast storm, he was greeted by Ngati Tumatakokiri warriors in canoes paddled from their pa on Taupo Point.

In the first contact between European and Maori, a misunderstanding of intentions led to four Dutch seamen in the ship's boat being speared and clubbed to death. The attack probably took place in Wainui Bay off Whariwharangi Beach. A sketch by Tasman's sailing master, who called the scene "Moordaerer's Bay", is all that Tasman recorded before hauling up anchor and sailing back to Batavia without ever setting foot on the land that Dutch charts named Nova Zeelandia.

The Ngati Tumatakokiri, who were displaced by invading northern tribes a century and a half later, seem to

have made even less of the encounter and Maori society remained unaffected by the contact.

When European explorers returned more than 100 years later they were the forerunner to succeeding waves of settlers who began to log the easily accessible Tasman Bay forests, build ships on the shore, quarry granite and marble, and clear hillsides to create pasture.

Perhaps fortunately for the walkers on the Abel Tasman Coastal Track the settlers' efforts ended when the easy timber was taken, and the hills left to gorse and bracken.

The ravaged landscape has slowly healed. Even huge blocks of marble cut from the Tonga Quarry and then abandoned on the beach appear almost like any other jumbled stack of bizarrely shaped granite that nature has fashioned and left on the foreshore.

There is a rich diversity of rock types in this small park that is surrounded by Tasman Bay and the vast Kahurangi National Park. But it is the physical and chemical qualities of the granite bedrock that dictate the forest cover and creates the texture and colour of beaches and streambeds.

The coast is a varied string of quiet coves, offshore islands, submerged reefs, caves and golden beaches embracing lazy lagoons. Golden granite is responsible for this treasured coast. Rainwater, slightly acidic with tannin leached from decaying forest vegetation, eats into weakened cracks left in the rock when it was first formed. The acid water separates the granite's mica, feldspar and quartz. The feldspar decomposes into soft clay but the hard quartz

crystals are washed down the rivers to be deposited along the coastline as magnificent golden beaches. In places crystalline rocks reflect from the shallow, azure water.

The landscape is at its most bizarre on the marble and schist terrace in the Canaan region. In this mountainous area on the western fringe of the park, centuries of a bitter rain has fluted outcrops of grey marble and hollowed out mountains into a honeycomb of caves and tunnels. Streams disappear into deep shafts, the deepest being the 176-metre Harwood's Hole.

In the 51km coastal track, much of it cut in the 1960s, there are signs of other forces at work too. The impact of timber milling, quarrying and farming is all evident in various places.

It should come as no surprise that the track, which can be walked by most people in a leisurely three to fives days, is extraordinarily popular: some 30,000 people walk all or part of the track each year. In the summer months its four huts are likely to be fully occupied so it pays to carry a tent to use on the 21 designated sites where camping is permitted.

Nelson's mild climate means it can be delightful tramping in the clear light of winter when the crowds have gone and waves tend to lap lonely beaches — and the track's notorious sandflies seem less hungry. The huts have heating and a water supply but walkers need to take their own portable stoves.

Sculptures in the sand of the Awaroa inlet.

There are several short walks off the main track to such features as the Cascade Falls (one hour) and Cleopatra's Pool (45 minutes). At Pitt Head, a short walk from Anchorage Hut, is the site of easily recognisable Maori fortifications. Scattered around are flakes of argillite, the debris left from toolmaking.

Offshore are a number of small islands that are free of introduced pests such as rats, possums and cats and provide a sanctuary for some rare native plants and animals.

Around Tonga Island is an extensive marine reserve where all marine life is totally protected. A breeding colony of New Zealand fur seals makes its home on the island. Male seals congregate between breeding seasons on Separation Point, a headland between Golden Bay and Tasman Bay that is easily reached as a short side trip from the track.

The several estuaries along the track are another feature of the Abel Tasman coast. Most are sandy rather than muddy, and their rich ecology can be easily explored. The nutrient-rich tide supports a wide range of marine and bird life.

The granite coasts are also alive with underwater flora and fauna. In these glassy waters there are stunning rewards for those who carry a diving mask and snorkel.

Previous page: **K**ayakers drift into the golden sand of a deserted lagoon on the Abel Tasman National Park coast just as sailors and canoeists have done for hundreds of years. The brilliant aquamarine sea and honey-coloured beach are exactly as nature created them.

A tramping family cool their feet in the clear waters of Onetahuti Beach, a spot at which to linger on day two of the Great Walk. Offshore lies distinctive Tonga Island, home to a colony of fur seals and part of a marine reserve where all marine life — including fish — are totally protected.

Sea kayaking around the Abel Tasman coastline is an increasingly popular way to fully appreciate the Abel Tasman coastal track. Commercial kayak companies give walkers the chance to paddle alongside the track on some days, exploring offshore islands and rocky outcrops, and sling their packs to tramp on other days.

ABEL TASMAN

T orrrent River, peaceful in the quiet of late afternoon, can catch unwary trampers who ignore the tides. An alternative track winds its way along the foreshore.

Overleaf: Golden sands and clear waters tend to dominate the Abel Tasman walk, yet always just a few metres inland, as here at Te Awaroa Bay, lies lush sub-tropical forest and cooling streams.

Above: **A**t low tide trampers can cross the estuary to Tonga Beach and pick up the track on the other side. Those who prefer dry feet can use an all-weather track at the top of the estuary. A granite quarry used to operate near here and huge blocks of granite, cut and discarded, lie on the beach.

A rocky sentinel, carved away by the sea, stands watch over the still waters of Anapai Bay. The bay, an easy 40-minute walk past the official end of the Great Walk at Totaranui, is a beautifully secluded spot to rest, swim or skindive. The track to it passes through a rainforest of ferns and palms.

HEAPHY

Giant granite boulders, shaped by a relentless Tasman Sea, lie on the beach on the coastal section of the Heaphy Track.

The 77km-long track crosses diverse landscapes before following the Heaphy River down to the roaring West Coast.

There can be a no more diverse, or leisurely, trek than the 77km Heaphy Track in the remote north-west of the South IslandThis Great Walk is rich in history, rich in the variety of terrain it covers, yet demanding only of an ambition to walk one of the most famous routes in New Zealand. Until the vast North West Nelson Forest Park was re-dedicated in 1996 as Kahurangi National Park, the thirteenth in New Zealand, the Heaphy could be comfortably ridden by mountainbikers.

National Park status gives the 452,000ha park over to walkers only but the bikers efforts have shown that the track is easy. In fact, the track is officially classified as a walk rather than a tramp and it can be completed in four to six days with comfortable huts no more than five hours' walking apart. River and stream crossings that once could be dangerous because of flash floods have now been bridged.

The diversity of landscape crossed by the Heaphy Track — and encompassed in Kahurangi National Park — is unequalled on other Great Walks. It ranges from forests of red and silver beech, tall podocarps with thick undergrowth, tannin-stained streams, alpine herb fields and the red tussock grasslands of the Gouland Downs, to the nikau palm groves on the mostly tempestuous West Coast.

Such is its standing that most people simply refer to the 100-year-old track as The Heaphy; when you have "done the

Heaphy", everyone knows that you are not referring to a river or mountain. You are talking about a journey from the junction of the Brown and Aorere Rivers, near Collingwood in Golden Bay, over tussock tops and lush forests to the mouth of the Heaphy River, then down the roaring West Coast to the Kohaihai River, 16km north of Karamea.

Charles Heaphy, the renowned explorer, artist and soldier from whom the track takes its name, travelled from Golden Bay to Westland, over what is now the coastal section of the Heaphy Track, in 1846.

At the time his epic four-month journey was one of the most arduous feats of exploration. But contrary to popular misconception Heaphy, a draughtsman with the New Zealand Company, and his companion, Thomas Brunner, a surveyor with the company, never ventured inland over the major part of the route that is now named after him.

In a way that is strange because Heaphy and Brunner had with them on their exploratory trip a Maori guide, Kehu. And for hundreds of years the Maori of Golden Bay had travelled to Westland to prospect for pounamu (greenstone) from which to fashion tools, weapons and ornaments.

The Maori had climbed up from the Aorere River, onto the forest-encircled plateau of the Gouland Downs where they could feast on weka (swamp hen), and down the Whakapoai (Heaphy) River to the treacherous coast north of the rivermouth. There they rounded huge bluffs using flax ladders and risked the wave-swept beaches.

An entry in Heaphy's diary indicated he was aware of the trail, but it wasn't until the discovery of gold in the Aorere Valley in 1856 that Europeans began exploring inland. The first to follow what is now the majority of the Heaphy Track is thought to be a goldminer named Aldridge who traversed it in 1859. A year later a government agent and warden on the Collingwood goldfields, James Mackay, followed the inland route home after buying almost the whole of the West Coast from the Maoris.

In 1862 Mackay cut the first "Heaphy Track" from the Aorere River to the mouth of the Heaphy. (It may have been more appropriate had the track been named after Mackay.)

Over the ensuing years it was developed as a pack-track by gold prospectors but by 1900 it had become overgrown, frequently blocked by slips and rarely used.

When the North West Nelson Forest Park was established in 1965 the track was cleared for public use.

In the 1970s the track was threatened by a proposal to build a road from Collingwood to the West Coast. The plan

Bizarre limestone outcrops intrude into the Heaphy Track high country.

was shelved and instead the former Forest Service improved the track facilities so that a route with a long tradition as a foot highway for trade and commerce would continue as one of the top tourist treks in the country.

The Heaphy can be walked both ways but most walkers travel northeast to southwest. From the 20-bunk Brown Hut at the road-end, 35km from the pleasant Golden Bay township of Collingwood, the track climbs steeply to the Perry Saddle, at 915m the highest point on the track.

On the climb up the head of the Aorere Valley it is possible on a clear day to see Mt Taranaki in the North Island.

From the Perry Saddle Hut the Heaphy sidles onto the tussock grasslands of the Gouland Downs — one of the oddest and most fascinating landscapes found on any of the Great Walks. In the dim light of dawn and dusk, or when there are storm clouds threatening, these otherwise magnificent red tussock hills are eerie and seemingly full of foreboding.

Geologically, this 3000ha fellfield, or eroded peneplain,

Scott's Beach, a good spot to rest before climbing the Kohaihai Saddle.

is possibly the most ancient in New Zealand with the sandstone and siltstone beneath the tussock about 400 to 500 million years old. The soil is thin and poor and only the tussock, some herbs and flaxes appear to grow. That is something of an illusion because there is actually a rich garden of herbs and flowers.

In summer there can be a profusion of colour as orchids (26 species), native lilies, gentians, and daisies burst into flower.

A total of 448 species of native plants, some of then rare, have been identified on the Gouland Downs. Prolific too are weka and kiwi, whose shrill screech is often heard at night.

A naturalist who visited the Downs in 1915 estimated there were 30,000 weka in the area, and several thousand great spotted kiwi. A disastrous grassland fire in 1938 devastated the population but the numbers appear to have recovered somewhat.

Another feature of the Downs are islands of limestone and ancient patches of beech forest that cling to them. Clinging to the beech is a fairyland of mosses, lichen and fern that gives these outcrops a mysterious and magical air.

From the Gouland Downs the track heads west on the margin between upland tussock grasslands and beech forest. From Mackay Hut it is possible to watch the sun setting over the Tasman Sea. The track then descends into luxuriant West Coast rain forest, where vines and epiphytes clasp giant podocarps, until it reaches the Heaphy River. A change in vegetation hardly has time to reveal the nearing West Coast before pounding surf can be heard.

Archaelogists have found evidence of moa hunter camps at the mouth of the Heaphy River. The 500-year-old site had been used extensively for producing tools and contained flakes of obsidian from Mayor Island in the Bay of Plenty. Charles Heaphy recorded seeing an overgrown potato ground near the river mouth, indicating it was a stopover point for Maori trading parties on the way to the greenstone fields further south.

The last stage of the Heaphy, 16km along the coast to the Kohaihai Shelter, is a dramatic juxtaposition of deafening surf and subtropical vegetation. Many walkers consider this section the highlight of their trip. It is also deceptively dangerous, and the sea has taken some lives; the risks can be avoided by using alternative high-tide tracks. Swimming is not recommended.

After tramping this section in the cold sea spray, a hot shower and soft bed are waiting at Karamea, only 16km from the track end at the Kohaihai Shelter.

Below: **A** handsome footbridge crosses the tannin-stained Kohaihai River at the end — or start — of the Heaphy Track.

Left: **T**he Heaphy Track may be walked in either direction. Trampers starting at the southern end begin at the Kohaihai River where there is a carpark, a shelter and a telephone with free calls to transport at Karamea 16km away.

Overleaf: **B**eneath the tussock grasslands of the Gouland Downs is the most ancient landform in New Zealand: sandstone and siltstone compacted some four to five hundred million years ago. Only red tussock, some herbs and flaxes can grow on the poor soil of this peneplain.

Below: **C**oastal shrubs and the red-flowering rata colour the red beech and rimu-forested hillsides.

HEAPHY

Right: **W**alkers take a welcome break at Saxon Hut on the Heaphy Track.

Below: The inviting sands of the West Coast can be hazardous for walking except at low tide. Rogue waves sweep up the sand without warning and undertows and rips make the sea unsafe for swimming.

HEAPHY

Right: The cool of a stream in the lush Heaphy forest where a walker might choose to rock hop across or risk the chill to ease sore feet.

Left and below: Thick groves of nikau, New Zealand's only native palm tree, face the pounding West Coast surf on the coastal sections of the Heaphy Track. Once the track followed a series of sandy beaches and rocky points but the 16km route was hazardous in rough conditions and the track now mostly avoids the beach sections.

HEAPHY

Overleaf: Footprints in the sand mark the final leg of the Heaphy Track. Leaning nikau palms and coastal shrubs on the steep hillsides bear testimony to the ferocity of the wind sweeping across the Tasman Sea.

ROUTEBURN

Wind, rain, cloud, and on a clear day the most beautiful views in the world. The Routeburn Track, the premier alpine trek in New Zealand, tends to capture all weathers, particularly above the bushline. Trampers scale the heights above Lake Mackenzie on a misty Routeburn day.

Decades ago New Zealand was infamous for its "six o'clock swill". The law then demanded that hotel public bars close at 6pm. So thirsty drinkers, with little time to spare after a day's work, packed the bars, bought huge amounts of beer, and swilled it down in an uncomfortably short time.

The outdoors had something similar in what may well have been dubbed the "Routeburn rush". Walkers on New Zealand's premier alpine trek, the three-day, 39km Routeburn Track, were known to leave one hut as early as 4am in an undignified rush to secure a bunk in the next hut. Having claimed their bed, they might spend most of the day guarding it from the hordes who followed — sometimes twice the number than there were bunks to hold them.

Fortunately, the six o'clock swill has vanished in the face of more civilised drinking hours, and the Routeburn rush has gone too with the introduction of a hut booking system by the Department of Conservation. What most definitely remains on the Routeburn, however, are the outstanding attractions that lure some 10,000 walkers a year.

It would be wrong to suggest that the Routeburn has everything, because it is far from the coast or any volcanic activity. Nor does it include the extensive tussock plateaus of the Heaphy. But as an alpine trek it is unsurpassed both in its own alpine herb fields, beech forests, alpine lakes and waterfalls, and in the panoramic views it provides of some of the most imposing ranges in the Southern Alps.

There are other reasons for the Routeburn's popularity, particularly among overseas tourists. At three days it is a convenient walk for many people. Its location is also convenient, starting near Glenorchy at the end of Lake Wakatipu, and a comfortable distance from other major treks in the Fiordland and Mt Aspiring National Parks.

The track straddles the Humboldt Mountains on the border of the two National Parks, passing through both of them. The route owes its origins to a centuries-old desire by travellers to get from the lake and valleys of Wakatipu across the Main Divide to the coast.

The first Routeburn walkers trekked up the Routeburn Valley about 500 years ago in search of pounamu (greenstone) which, in the absence of iron, was invaluable for making tools, weapons and ornaments. The Maori called what is now the Routeburn Te Komana and it was an important trade route between the coast and Lake Wakatipu; the traditional directions for the trail were memorised in song. The last greenstone-collecting expedition across the Routeburn is believed to have been held in 1852.

The first European settlers were quick to appreciate the Maori's path-finding skills. Early runholders explored the approaches to the route but it was the Otago goldrush and the discovery of the precious metal in the Dart River by Patrick Caples in 1863 that led to the trail being re-opened.

The gold was a tortuously long way from Dunedin, the provincial centre. If it could be taken to the coast at Martins Bay along a route rumoured to be used by the Maori traders, it could then be easily shipped to Dunedin.

Caples, a member of the Otago Mining Board, set out with his dog to discover the route. He climbed the Routeburn

Valley and onto the Harris Saddle from where he could see that the Hollyford River led to Martins Bay. Settlement of Martins Bay began in 1870 along with grandiose plans of roads linking the settlement with Queenstown. But the bay proved a death-trap for shipping and, along with the half-completed bridle trail, the settlement was soon abandoned.

It might well have stayed that way but for the Bryant family of Kinloch, a landing place on the shores of Lake

Above: **Home is a backcountry hut.**

Right: **Sidling around the tussock tops.**

Wakatipu, who saw the potential of the overgrown route as a tourist track.

The fortunes of the track waxed and waned for nearly 40 years until it become firmly established as a premier tourist route. Nowadays the track is a sort of two-in-one in that there are huts for independent walkers, maintained by either the Aspiring or Fiordland National Parks, and a complementary series of huts — complete with hot showers — for the guided clients of Routeburn Walk Ltd.

The park huts have gas cookers and heaters, cold water and flush toilets, and during the busy season there is a hut warden present. As well, more than a dozen different nationalities and just as many languages are likely to be present.

New Zealanders make up just 25 per cent of the walkers, a fact that could have caused some resentment in the days of the Routeburn rush when it was necessary to queue for almost everything from scrubbing a billy to going to the toilet.

Now the only resentment is directed to those who ignore their share of hut chores such as sweeping out the bunk room

and wiping down the bench before leaving. Backcountry hut ethics require that they be left as clean and tidy as possible.

Because this is New Zealand, it is also quite possible to find yourself sharing the track with someone like the Prime Minister, Mr Jim Bolger, and his family trekking on a summer holiday.

Outside of the peak of the season it is actually possible to find the track almost deserted, but negotiating this alpine route in winter can be dangerous for all but experienced and well-equipped trampers.

The highest section of the track near Lake Harris is under

snow for six months of the year and can be hazardous in summer too. In 1963, two 13-year-old school children caught in a blizzard on the tops died from hypothermia.

The rain in these regions is notorious. Fiordland averages 200 raindays a year and falls of 250mm a day, and continuing for days on end, are not uncommon. Yet when the sun shines on the Routeburn it brightens a microcosm of all that is best in the South Island outdoors and its walking tracks.

It is no real surprise to find that a book devoted to the great treks of the world should choose the Routeburn as its New Zealand entry.

The justification begins even before the track because Glenorchy and the appropriately named Paradise area, around the confluence of the Dart and Rees rivers, is quite simply one of the most beautiful spots you can visit in New Zealand without even having to step out of a motor vehicle. Above the pastureland are deep green slopes of beech forest rising to grand snow-capped peaks like Earnslaw, the monarch of Wakatipu.

The Glenorchy end of the track begins not far away at the Routeburn Shelter, across the Dart River bridge and 75km from Queenstown. The track follows the Routeburn Valley and its braided river, through beech forest to the snow tussock tops on the Harris Saddle where Mt Cook lillies bloom in random clumps.

On the 1277m-high saddle the terrain is rough and patches of snow linger for a long time. The heavily glaciated slopes and sheer rock walls of the Darran Mountains — famed for alpine rock climbing — provide a backdrop that leaves even fit walkers panting. Soaring above all are Mt Madeline and Tutoko, the highest mountains in Fiordland.

At times the Routeburn has suffered from the weight of foot traffic, particularly in areas of peat bogs, but in recent years much work has been done to bridge streams and construct boardwalks over swamps and around bluffs. Most of the track now is broad, dry and comfortable with huts or shelters never more than three hours' walking apart. And the crowds? Anyone looking at the Darrans will never notice them.

Previous page: **I**n early winter the view from the Routeburn Falls Hut is stunning as new snow covers the mountain tops and dusts the beech forests above the braided Routeburn River flats. North Branch enters the main Routeburn to the left.

Below: **B**oardwalks are constructed across marshy areas to protect fragile alpine flora from the tramping of too many feet.

ROUTEBURN

Right: **W**ater that begins its journey high in the mountains saturates the bush near the lowland start to the Routeburn Track.

Below: **A** rocky promontory just below the huts at Routeburn Falls is an ideal place to sunbathe away aches and pains and admire the magnificent view down the Routeburn Valley.

ROUTEBURN

Left: **A** number of suspension bridges span the lower Routeburn. The boulders around which water roars and foams may have been carried from high in the hills by powerful floods, or left exposed by retreating glaciers.

Overleaf: **A** steep climb above Lake Harris is through rough alpine terrain, but even when cloud hangs on the tops the views make every arduous step worthwhile.

Below: Routeburn Flats open out to reveal a wide, grassy valley. Mt Somnus can be seen on a clear day and in the alpine quiet can be heard the gentle sound of birdsong and the tumbling river.

Above: On the rocky knoll of Key Summit, easily reached in half an hour from Lake Howden Hut, lies a beautiful alpine tarn and a superb view of the imposing peaks of the Darrans. On the far left skyline are the three distinct peaks, Ngatimamoe, Flat Top Peak and Pyramid Peak.

Overleaf: Lake Howden Hut nestling on the lake foreshore is near the busy intersection of the Routeburn and Greenstone tracks, close to the Key Summit track and the Milford and Hollyford roads.

MILFORD

Waterfalls tumbling down into glacial valleys, such as Mackay Falls pcitured, are the unmistakable signature of the Milford Track, a tourist route across the Alps for more than 100 years.

If this is the finest walk in the world where is everyone? The thought is inescapable on the Milford Track, the 55km trek from Lake Te Anau to Milford Sound that has been luring walkers for more than 100 years.

On any one day in the walking season there are at least 245 people somewhere on this Fiordland trail. Yet it is possible to walk from morning to dusk in almost splendid isolation. In front and behind, the track appears deserted, fallen leaves are barely disturbed and a thin layer of moss covers rocks that lie like flagstones in the path.

This is, after all, the Milford Track, the route that in 1903 the fledgling Department of Tourist and Health Resorts billed as a "tourist foot road" to Milford; now 11,000 pairs of feet are reputed to make the trip each year. Yet it looks as though

Scottish surveyor Quinton Mackinnon blazed his trail up the Clinton valley from the head of Lake Te Anau only yesterday.

On a bleak rainy day on 17 October 1888, Mackinnon struggled over the pass that now bears his name, six weeks after setting out from Te Anau, and down the Arthur Valley into Milford Sound.

Mackinnon had a well-honed entrepreneurial streak and he wasn't thinking much of colonists or the government's commission to find an overland route into Milford Sound. Another Scot, Donald Sutherland, had set up a painters' retreat in Milford Sound and Mackinnon immediately saw the potential for tourism in the route he had forged.

Within months Mackinnon was guiding tourists along his track. Twenty-four years later a British travel writer and poet, Blanche Baughan, labelled Mackinnon's walk the finest in the world and people have been coming in droves ever since. So where are they?

The secret to the Milford Track, and it is one that many who have never walked it do not appreciate, is that people can only walk the track one way and the numbers on it are restricted to the number of hut bunks available.

So everyone walks at their own pace, never needing to pass another on the trail. And when walkers do meet up, perhaps while stopping to take a photograph, it will only be another bend in the trail or a brief pause to stare before you find yourself alone again.

If there is one other special feature of the Milford it is the likely frequency of photographic stops. The track is basically two glacially carved valleys back to back, separated by the 1073m high Mackinnon Pass across the Main Divide. With the benefit of a track to follow, it seems a fairly obvious route. It is also scenically stunning.

Every bend in the track seems to reveal another feature of the gin-clear Clinton or Arthur Rivers and the mountains crowding in on them that demands a photograph be taken.

Mackinnon was despatched over the mountains for something a little more mundane. He was supposed to find an overland route for road or rail to a West Coast port that would effectively link Otago with Australia.

One of the ironies of the track is that in years to come tourists on cruise ships visiting Milford Sound would often make a special trip to see the Sutherland Falls, at 580m the highest in New Zealand.

The falls are the source of one of those historic vignettes too because it is alleged that Sutherland and fellow explorer John Mackay travelled up the Arthur Valley in 1877 in search of gold. After naming the Mackay Falls near the head of Lake Ada, it was agreed that the next falls they reached would be given Sutherland's name.

Until 1954 it was necessary to walk the track both ways, but completion of the Homer tunnel and opening of the Milford road enabled the track to become a point-to-point route.

The Milford has huts for freedom walkers and huts for commercially guided treks. There is something agreeably indulgent about hot showers at the end of the day and someone else to cook the evening meal.

By rights it should make for a "them-and-us" situation on the track but on the occasions that guided walkers and freedom walkers meet up, such as on Mackinnon Pass, there is usually nothing but good fellowship.

The environment is so overwhelming that any

Stands of beech forest near the lower reaches of the Clinton River make a comforting start to the Milford Track.

differences over the size of a pack or the comfort of a bed seem fairly trivial.

Both lots of walkers begin their journey on the same Te Anau launch — and end it on the same launch to Milford too. The first two days walking lie up the immense Clinton Canyon. Its steep walls were cut by a glacier 15,000 years ago and somewhere out of sight on their tops are catchments for snow and the rainfall that can total a staggering 8000mm a year.

At times the snow can crash down as an avalanche but the most common aftermath of the frequent rain — and subject of many photographs — are dozens of pencil-thin waterfalls gushing down cracks in the rockface.

The Clinton River is perfectly clear and it is not unusual

The Clinton River widens as it nears Lake Te Anau. Ahead lies the Clinton Canyon and the track to Milford Sound.

to see trout lazily circling in some of the pools.

Near Lake Mintaro, source of the Clinton, the track passes through a Tolkein forest of moss-draped fuchsia before beginning a zigzag climb to the top of the pass. In the spring there are large clumps of mountain daisies and mountain buttercups in flower on the side of the trail.

Mackinnon Pass is not much more than a football field across but it can be bitterly exposed and there is a large shelter there to warm chilled bodies. There is also a toilet with one of the best views in Fiordland — right down the floor of the Clinton Canyon towards Te Anau.

The Arthur Valley, nearly 900m below the pass, tends to be more open, particularly when it nears Milford Sound. Sutherland Falls, fifth highest in the world, is near its head and walkers who don't mind getting

drenched can walk behind the roaring water veil and out the other side.

In 1890 an intrepid young surveyor, Will Quill, climbed to the top of the falls and discovered the reservoir that bears his name. Sadly he fell to his death a year later while trying to negotiate Gertrude Saddle a few kilometres away.

The last day on the Milford Track is the longest but the rewards are to cross rushing mountain streams near several beautiful waterfalls.

Lake Ada is well stocked with trout and those who have had no luck on the Clinton can always hire a guide at the Boatshed and troll for a consolation catch.

Sandfly Point and a sign festooned with discarded tramping boots is the official end of the track but a launch is needed to get to Milford. That seems an appropriate way to end this track because it was Milford Sound — actually a fiord rather than a sound — that was the reason for the track in the first place.

Mitre Peak, the sound's trademark, deserves to be the last photograph in any collection on the Milford Track — the finest walk in the world.

Previous page: The Clinton River running into Lake Te Anau is the initial pathway to Milford Sound, the route of the famed Milford Track. At Clinton Forks, clearly visible in the top left, the track follows the West Branch of the river, along Clinton Valley.

MILFORD

Below: A feature of the track is its proximity to the rivers flowing along the ancient glacial valleys that the trail follows.

Right: Dozens of waterfalls tumbling off the tops into the Clinton Canyon are a spectacular feature of the Milford Track.

Below: Lake Mintaro, nestling at the foot of the Mackinnon Pass, is the site of a Department of Conservation Hut for freedom walkers.

MILFORD

Right: In spring the giant mountain buttercups, or Mt Cook lilies, lie beside the trail.

Left: **F**ew people walk the Milford Track without bravely perching for a photograph on Mackinnon Pass, several hundred metres above Quinton Hut.

MILFORD

Above: **M**ackinnon memorial cairn on the 1073m heights of Mackinnon Pass, with Mt Hart in the background. From now on it is downhill all the way to Milford Sound.

Overleaf: **M**ackinnon Pass and a chance to look back on the route so far — the Clinton Valley stretching all the way back to Lake Te Anau.

Left: **S**utherland Falls, highest in the land, plunge 580 metres in three successive leaps down the sheer rock face, from their origin in Lake Quill.

MILFORD

Above: **S**haded by the mountains and soaked by an extraordinary rainfall, the forest understorey is often a lush goblin forest of lichen and moss.

Overleaf: **T**he Arthur River, which feeds Milford Sound with fresh mountain water, carves the route west for Milford Track walkers.

Above: **A**ptly named Mitre Peak, trademark of Milford   Sound, stands about halfway along the sound on the southern shore, and provides a beacon for the conclusion of the Milford Track.

Left: **F**rom the jetty at Sandfly Point it is just a short launch trip to the settlement of Milford Sound.

KEPLER

Walkers on the Kepler Track climb onto the mountain tops on a purpose-built trekking highway.

They run the Kepler Track. Every year hardy athletes and many social runners complete the 67km Kepler Challenge Mountain Run. Some run in under five hours, some almost crawl in up to 11 hours. There are youngsters and there are people touching 70. Regardless, what they do says a lot about a Great Walk through the Fiordland wilderness that is normally tramped in four days.

The Kepler, which traverses the edges of Lakes Te Anau and Manapouri and climbs to 1200m on exposed alpine ridges, is a modern track, constructed in the 1980s to try to take some pressure off the older tracks in the region.

The New Zealand Tourist and Publicity Department provided funding, and Operation Raleigh, the international organisation that assists with youth projects around the world, organised some labour. Those were probably the easy items. In

the Kepler Mountains in the vast Fiordland National Park it rains, and rains.

Water shapes the land and makes building a track through its waterlogged valleys a frustrating and difficult endeavour. Putting a track through the beech forests on the valley floors involved digging drains, hauling dead trees out of the way, cutting through roots, building boardwalks across bogs and shovelling load after wheelbarrow load of gravel.

About 40 Department of Conservation staff and the Operation Raleigh volunteers spent six months on the track working in shifts of 10 days on, four days off. Conditions were so bad with rain and fog that sometimes workers could only see as far as their hands. Before the track was even open it had to be shifted in the vicinity of Dock Bay, on Lake Te Anau, because the track builders' first effort lay under water. Lake Te Anau rose to its highest level in 10 years just to show the track makers that in

Fiordland it is not wise to take nature for granted.

Temperatures can drop 20 degrees in a few hours; a hot nor'-wester in the morning may be followed by blizzard conditions and snow in the afternoon. And the storms that arrive literally out of the blue may depart just as quickly. It could be worse. The Keplers are on the leeward side of the Main Divide and receive less rain than other parts of Fiordland.

The track was opened in February 1988 as part of the National Park Centennial Year celebrations. It shows its relative youth: compared to many other walking tracks in the country it has been built to a high standard. The walking gradient is always easy, and there is a generous provision of bridges, and boardwalks keep feet dry. As well, the track forms a complete circuit so while the landscape it traverses has some similarities with other walking routes nearby, the transport arrangements for walkers are usually easier to organise.

Purpose-built it might be, but the Kepler has an honourable history. While the area surrounding the track has never seen much settlement, it has seen centuries of foot traffic as groups of Maori hunted birds or fished for eels in the valleys and streams. And from villages on the Waiau River and at Te Anau trading parties passed through the area on their way to Milford to collect a type of jade.

The surveyor James McKerrow, who named many of the track's features, was one of the early European visitors to the Kepler Mountains.

There have been attempts at farming the slopes of Mt Luxmore with sheep, and populating it with skiers — there are the remains of an old towrope on Mt Luxmore — but the ridges and river valleys seem to have found their most lasting role as a venue for walkers. Within two months of the track opening in 1988 it had seen 2000 visitors.

The farming attempts on Luxmore, where there is now a 40-bunk hut, are remembered on maps by the notation "Beer's Farm". Jack Beer farmed the area from about 1890 until his death in 1930 at the age of 70. He had around 700 sheep and used to shear them wherever he could catch them. He cut a

track through the bush so his flock could graze on the grassy tops of Mt Luxmore during the summer months, but the Kepler Track builders could not locate it.

Te Anau locals tell a tale of Jack Beer collecting a sack of flour from the Te Anau Hotel and carrying it home. When he found it was addressed to someone else he immediately carried it back again.

Another Jack Beer story has him pushing a pig in a wheelbarrow 21km to a farm at Lake Manapouri. When the

Left: The track crosses several dark, shady gullies full of ferns and mosses. Dense groups of crown fern predominate in the forest understorey.

Right: Below Mt Luxmore the Kepler is benched on a comfortable gradient.

farmer wouldn't buy it, Beer pushed the beast on to Te Anau. Beer used to keep the distinctive Banded Berkshire breed. His pigs eventually became wild and were known by local hunters as "Beer's meat".

In a small way the Kepler Track is a legacy to the early runholders like Beer because it was recreational walkers following in their tracks who gave the impetus to develop a new trek in the vast Fiordland National Park. Some older routes were included with the 67km Kepler Track.

The Keplers are on the eastern fringe of the park. To the north is the Murchison Range and to the south the Hunter Mountains. Lake Te Anau, second largest in New Zealand, and Lake Manapouri complete the quadrants.

The track makes use of all the geographical features of Fiordland, including lake-edge strolls, tramping through beech forest and climbing onto open tops, and along valleys carved by glaciers thousands of years ago.

Getting to the start of the Kepler couldn't be easier. There

are regular shuttle services from Te Anau — or a 45-minute walk from park headquarters in the town — to the control gates from Lake Manapouri.

The track follows the lake shore and passes through beech and kamahi forest, with a succulent understorey, before reaching Brod Bay. Day walkers often follow this section and make use of a water ferry service back to Te Anau.

From Brod Bay the track climbs through beech forest, past weathered limestone bluffs and emerges on the snow tussock on the flanks of Mt Luxmore and spectacular views across Lake Te Anau.

The Luxmore is one of three huts on the track — there is a smaller hut at Shallow Bay, Lake Te Anau — which by New Zealand standards are equipped to an extraordinary degree. In summer the huts, which sleep about 50 people, have gas cooking and heating, running water, and flush toilets.

Mt Luxmore at 1471m is the lowest on the Kepler Range, with 1696m Spire Peak, west of Iris Burn, the highest. Some 30 million years ago these peaks were at sea level and in the conglomerate rock they are made of can be found the fossils of sea shells.

Mt Luxmore Hut sits somewhat below the summit at 1085m but there is a marked track to the top of the peak. From there to the Hanging Valley Shelter is across the tops and considerably exposed. This section is the longest ridge walk of any of the Great Walks and the views across Fiordland are stunnng.

In contrast the Iris Burn Valley, where the next hut is located, is a grassy river valley surrounded by beech and podocarp forest; only a short walk from the hut is the refreshing Iris Burn waterfall.

The Iris Burn is a typical glacial U-shaped valley and the track climbs over a moraine hill before starting down it. Not far down the valley is the site of a huge slip in 1984 which flattened the vegetation on the forest floor.

Moturau Hut on the beachfront of Lake Manapouri is the third hut on the Kepler. The lake was the focus of a major environmental battle in the 1960s and 1970s. Plans to raise the lake level to increase electricity generation production were successfully opposed.

The biggest problem on the lake shore now is likely to be voracious sandflies.

From Moturau the track follows the Waiau River, a renowned trout fishing water, back to the control gates at Te Anau — and the town that calls itself the "walking capital of New Zealand" without much fear of contradiction.

Previous page: The Kepler Track, beginning on the shores of Lake Te Anau, climbs through beech forest and high into the Alps on a route that encapsulates almost every facet of South Island flora, fauna and geology.

KEPLER

There is less than a day's walking between the Te Anau township and the Mt Luxmore Hut on the other side of the lake, but by the time you get there it might as well be a world away.

Right: Easy going across exposed ridgetops and a fine view too.

Previous page: Iris Burn runs quietly, serenely from Iris Burn Falls to Lake Manapouri through forest that is a haven for native birds. Walkers usually meander along the track, never out of earshot of the tinkling burn.

KEPLER

Right: Cosy Iris Burn Hut on the valley floor sleeps about 60 people. It is just a short stroll to the Iris Burn waterfall. At dusk brown kiwi can be heard calling on the flats.

The track passes beneath massive limestone bluffs, fluted by rainwater and overhanging in places. Mosses, native stinging nettles and small shrubs find a home in the cracks and around the base of the crags.

Overleaf: Just before the track zigzags into Hanging Valley a side track leads to a spectacular viewpoint above Iris Burn. On a clear day the whole valley is visible as far as Lake Manapouri.

RAKIURA

On Stewart Island the sea touches almost everything and everyone, including trampers on the Rakiura Great Walk. In a quiet bay near Oban and the start-finish of the walk, the evidence of a maritime community sits gently at its moorings.

Passports are not needed to cross to Stewart Island. If they were, it might reveal an interesting story because New Zealand's third main island seems better known to foreigners than to New Zealanders.

Most visitors are young backpackers who probably decide that having already come to near the end of the world they might as well venture 27km across Foveaux Strait and complete the journey.

What they find on Te Punga o te Waka a Maui, the anchorstone of the South Island, is an island very much in its own right; a place sufficiently different from the rest of the country as to more than warrant the effort to get there.

Surprisingly, the 60km-long island is part of the same warped and mostly submerged mass of granite that forms some of Fiordland. But the island has been isolated for so long, and its soils and climate sufficiently different, that most of its vegetation is significantly changed from related species on the South Island.

Visiting backpackers tend to be enticed initially by the Rakiura Track, a Great Walk given the traditional Maori name for the island. Rakiura means "glowing skies": at its extreme southern latitudes daylight lasts longer and the skies glow from pale grey to sharp blue and bright orange.

The 165,000ha island wasn't always so isolated. The extent of New Zealand's dry land has varied over millions of years and was at its greatest during the last ice age when the country, including Stewart Island, was one land mass.

Nearly 20,000 years later the Maori found it was an anchorstone but European navigator Captain James Cook took

Sydney Cove beach and Ulva Island, two gems of Paterson Inlet.

a punt and mistook the island for a peninsula. William Stewart got it right in the early 1800s and modestly called the roughly triangular-shaped island after himself.

Since then it has been like most small islands — isolated and ignored. Rakiura deserves better and, thanks mainly to tourism, is slowly getting it.

If crossing Foveaux Strait, where the locals rate three-metre waves a gentle chop, on a high-speed catamaran from Bluff begins as reason enough to tick off another destination, it usually doesn't end that way.

Virtually the only settlement is Oban at Halfmoon Bay, and as picturesque as its Scottish namesake. The loose township of about 500 people has a general store, a hotel, a backpackers lodge, a couple of cafes, a Department of Conservation visitor centre — and more than 30,000 visitors a year.

With just 20km of roading on the island it is a walker's paradise; a place where tourists walk without fear, kayak, fish perhaps, or relax in an unhurried and unspoiled environment.

An encouragement to walk is the 250km of tracks and 21 Department of Conservation huts and shelters on the island. The various tracks make a rough circuit of the northern half of the island and encompass most of its diverse scenery.

Paterson Inlet, and its many arms, are the main incentive for sea kayaking. The inlet penetrates the milder north-east coast to half the width of the island. The inlet has a chequered history; its sheltered anchorages were once regularly used by whaling fleets. Now sea kayakers may share it with blue penguins and, perhaps, a pod of bottlenose dolphins.

The inlet has been filled with water since the last ice age and is home to many seabirds. At its head are the Freshwater River flats and the Rakeahua Wetlands, both areas of outstanding botanical interest.

Ulva Island in the middle of the inlet was once the hub of the community. There was a post office there for 50 years and when mail arrived a flag would be raised to signal sawmillers, fishermen and farmers to come and collect it.

Possums and whitetail deer have made an impact on the Stewart Island flora but rabbits, stoats and ferrets have never been introduced so the bird population thrives. Tui, kaka, fernbird and parakeet are all common and the island is the only place in New Zealand where spotting a kiwi in daytime is not at all unusual. The Stewart Island brown kiwi are recognised as a distinct species, and are usually seen in the unusual habitat of dunes and tussock grasslands.

The forest cover of Rakiura is unusual too because it lacks the predominant beech found in the South Island.

The 36km Rakiura Track can be walked in either direction and at any time of the year. It takes no more than three days to complete and the highest point is just 300m.

As with most places in New Zealand, timber milling was a substantial early industry. The remains of old boilers and the off-cut waste from sawmills are not uncommon. Between Kaipipi Bay and Halfmoon Bay the old road that serviced the mills is part of the track.

Maori Beach, one of the first to be reached on the track, had a thriving settlement until early this century and is one of the many historic places on the island.

Sealers, whalers and gold seekers followed the early Maori settlers to this all-weather anchorage. Port William Hut and an old wharf are all that remain of a grandiose scheme to settle 1000 people along the north-east coast to develop an oyster industry. Barracks were built for 150 people and 24 Shetlanders arrived in 1873 but soon departed. Their only legacy is a grove of mature eucalyptus trees near the hut.

Toward North Arm Hut the large sections of the boggy track have been covered by boardwalks. There is a lush forest in this area of high rainfall with some huge rimu and rata trees.

The relatively new section of track between North Arm Hut and Kaipipi Bay was built to give walkers the chance to be near the shore and beaches of Paterson Inlet.

The birdlife is prolific: fantails, bellbirds and native pigeons, and in the estuaries oyster catchers, herons and gulls.

By far the commonest bird species are petrels; one species, the sooty shearwater, generally known as the muttonbird, is prized for eating. The birds nest in burrows on some islets off Stewart Island after migrating across the Pacific. Fledglings are taken in their thousands and preserved in their own fat in containers made from bull kelp leaves. The Maori who sold Rakiura in 1863 retained an exclusive right to harvest the birds.

Codfish, one of the mutton bird islands, has become vitally important as one of the predator-free sanctuaries where it is hoped that the kakapo will breed. The unique ground parrot is at present close to extinction.

The barren and bleak heights to the south of Stewart Island do not lie on the Great Walk but they are worth detouring to look at. Here are huge granite lumps and mini-mountains, polished smooth and shiny by some ancient glacier. From a distance the feldspar crystals in the granite shine like glass.

If there is one enduring memory of Stewart Island, however, it is likely to be a kiwi, jumping onto the track ahead of you in broad daylight and calmly walking on ahead for several minutes before again disappearing into the scrub.

That, perhaps, is a reminder of Stewart Island's difference and unique unspoilt beauty.

Previous page: **H**alfmoon Bay and the settlement of Oban around its shores is the picturesque beginning to a genuine "away from it all" adventure.

RAKIURA

Below: **A** sea kayaker rests at Ulva Island in Paterson Inlet. Native birds are abundant on the island and an elephant seal may be found resting on rocks on the beach. Kayaks are readily available for hire and Rakiura walkers can mix a little paddling with their tramping.

Above: **I**n many places the track follows the shore, skirting the coastal dunes.

Overleaf: **T**he Maori called Stewart Island the anchor stone of Maui's canoe. These granite knobs on the range that overlooks the Rakiura track seem to fit the description.

Below: The Rakiura Great Track can be even greater for those with time to extend their journey by taking in the north-west and southern circuits. On the southern track the route between Mason Bay and Doughboy Bay often skirts the foreshore.

RAKIURA

Left: On the North Arm of Paterson Inlet the track has been boardwalked to protect the damp understory of the coastal forest from erosion.

Overleaf: The rugged north coast of Stewart Island.

Mason Bay — perhaps the most southerly spot in New Zealand that a tramper might stand and stare at the sun forcing its way through storm clouds.

Acknowledgements

The publishers would like to acknowledge the assistance of the many people and companies who contributed photographs to this book. In particular, thanks must go to Gareth Eyres, Exposure, for allowing us access to his vast collection of work.

The following photo libraries have all contributed greatly to this publication:

Andris Apse, DAC, Focus, FotoPacific, Full Frame, Go Wild Photography, International Press Photo Library, Key Light, Visual Impact, Treble Court Photography

Photographs are credited below to the individual photographer, where they are known.

Gareth Eyres, Exposure: p. 4 & 5, 6 & 7, 8, 16 & 17, 18, 33 (bottom), 34 & 35, 48, 49, 50 & 51, 52 & 53, 54 (top), 55, 56 & 57 (top), 57 (bottom), 58 & 59, 60 & 61 (top), 61 (bottom), 62 & 63, 80, 81, 88, 89 (top), 92 & 93 (top), 92 (bottom), 93 (bottom), 94 & 95, 114 & 115 (top), 116, 117, 118, 120 & 121,122 (top), 123; **Nathan Secker:** p. 1, 9, 11, 14 & 15, 87; **Craig Potton:** p. 10, 72, 74; **Geoff Mason:** p. 12, 33 (top); **Denis Page:** p. 13, 82, 83, 86 (bottom); **NZ Herald:** p. 19; **Full Frame:** p. 20, 21 (top), 134 & 135, 136 (top); **John Barkla** p. 21 (bottom), 22 & 23, 36 & 37, 42 (bottom), 43, 47; **Cam Feast:** p. 24, 25 (bottom), 26 & 27, 66; **DAC:** p. 2 & 3, 25 (top), 40 & 41, 42 (top), 69 (bottom), 70 & 71, 100, 101, 102 (top); **Hugh van Noorden:** p. 28 (top), 137, 138, 139 & 140; **Colin Moore:** p. 28 (bottom), 32, 111 (top), 114 (bottom); **Brian Enting:** p. 29, 30 & 31; **Rae Acherman:** p. 38, 39, 43 (top); **Stephen Jones:** p. 43, 44 & 45; **Les Molloy:** p. 46, 137 (bottom), 138 & 139; **Grant Hunter:** p 54 (bottom),105; **Nic Bishop:** p. 64, 65, 76, 77 (bottom), 78 & 79, 124 & 125, 126 (top); **Roger Fowler:** p. 67, 75; **Gaylene Earl:** p. 69 (top); **Andris Apse:** p. 84 & 85, 86 (top), 89 (bottom), 90 & 91, 104, 107 (bottom), 108 & 109, 111 (bottom), 111 & 112, 132, 140; **Brian Moorhead:** p. 68, 77 (top), 126 (bottom), 127 (bottom), 128 & 129; **Gottlieb Braun-Elwert:** p. 73; **John Blackwell:** p. 96, 97, 99; **Sheena Haywood:** p. 102 (bottom), 110; **Ian Kelly:** p. 103; **Hamish Angus:** p. 106; **Horizon/Trevor Dawes:** p. 107 (top); **Rob Greenaway:** p. 119, 122 (bottom), 127 (top), 130, 131, 136 (bottom)

ISBN 1-86958-314-0

© Text: Hodder Moa Beckett Ltd
© Photographs: as credited

Published in 1996 by Hodder Moa Beckett Publishers Limited
[a member of the Hodder Headline Group]
4 Whetu Place, Mairangi Bay, Auckland, New Zealand

Printed through Bookbuilders Ltd, Hong Kong